FIFTY YEARS AGO
At Home

Karen Bryant-Mole

WAYLAND

Titles in the series
At Home
Going on a Trip
Having Fun
In the High Street

All Wayland books encourage children to read and help them improve their literacy.

✓ The contents page, page numbers, headings and index help locate specific pieces of information.

✓ The glossary reinforces alphabetic knowledge and extends vocabulary.

✓ The further information section suggests other books dealing with the same subject.

✓ Find out more about how this book is specifically relevant to the National Literacy Strategy on page 31.

Editor: Carron Brown
Consultant: Norah Granger
Cover design: White Design
Inside design: Michael Leaman
Photo stylist: Gina Brown
Production controller: Carol Titchener

First published in 1998 by
Wayland Publishers Limited,
61 Western Road, Hove,
East Sussex BN3 1JD

© Copyright 1998 Wayland Publishers Limited

Typeset in England by Michael Leaman
Colour Separation by P&W Graphics, Singapore
Printed and bound in Italy by L.G. Canale &
C.S.p.A, Turin

British Library Cataloguing in Publication Data
Bryant-Mole, Karen
  At home. – (Fifty years ago)   1. Family –
  Great Britain – History – 20th century –
  Juvenile literature. 2. Great Britain Social
   conditions – 1945 – Juvenile literature.
  3. Great Britain – Social life and customs –
  1945 – Juvenile literature.
  I. Title 941'. 085

ISBN 0 7502 2265 4

Picture acknowledgements
The publishers would like to thank
the following for allowing their pictures
to be used in this book: Corbis 9, 25;
Getty Images *cover* [main] 5, 7, 11, 21; Robert
Harding 13, 17; Topham 15, 19, 23, 27; Wayland
Picture Library/Angela Hampton *cover* [inset], 4,
5, 6, 7, 8, 10, 11, 12, 14, 16, 18, 20, 22, 24, 26.

CONTENTS

In this book we are introduced to the Taylor family. We will meet Mr and Mrs Taylor, their children Luke and Sophie, and Luke and Sophie's grandparents Stan and Maureen. Compare their life at home today to family life at home fifty years ago.

WASHING CLOTHES

This washing machine fills itself with water.

Mr Taylor will add the washing powder, choose the wash programme he wants to use and then press the start button. When the clothes are washed, the machine will spin out most of the water.

This woman's washing machine was filled with water from a tap.

Few people had washing machines fifty years ago. They had to wash everything by hand. When they had washed their clothes they put them through a mangle to squeeze out the water.

I remember...

Maureen Taylor is Luke and Sophie's grandmother. She remembers the wash days in her house. 'My mum used to keep her washing machine in a cupboard. It had little wheels underneath it. When she wanted to use it, she pushed it over to the sink. You had to push the clothes around by hand.'

IRONING

Mrs Taylor is pouring water into her steam iron.

Mrs Taylor can choose whether she wants her iron to be hot or cool. She uses different temperatures for different types of material. She uses steam to help get any creases out of the clothes. The Taylor family have some clothes that do not need to be ironed.

This woman used a dry iron.

It was quite difficult to get creases out of clothes with an iron like this. It was easier to iron clothes when they were slightly damp. Fifty years ago, almost all clothes had to be ironed.

I remember...

Stan remembers his mum hanging out the washing on a clothes line in the yard. 'My mum said the wind blew most of the creases out and made the clothes easier to iron. After the clothes were ironed, she hung them on a clothes horse which she stood in front of the coal fire, to let the clothes air.'

Mr Taylor is putting a ready-prepared meal into the microwave.

Mr Taylor sometimes has to work quite late. If he wants a meal in a hurry, he takes some food out of the freezer and cooks it in the microwave. The Taylors also use an electric cooker for cooking.

This little girl helped her mum with the cooking.

Fifty years ago, there was a shortage of some kinds food. This was because of the Second World War which had ended in 1945. Many kinds of food were very expensive, so people did a lot of baking at home.

I remember...

Maureen remembers helping her mum in the kitchen. 'I learned everything I know about cooking from my mum. She also taught me not to waste food. Left-over meat would be minced up and made into pies. Bones would be boiled and the liquid used for soup. It was always mum who did the cooking.'

MEAL TIMES

Luke and Sophie usually have their tea before their dad gets home from work.

Luke and Sophie are having pizza at tea-time. Pizza is Sophie's favourite meal. Luke prefers pasta with a chicken sauce.

This family ate Sunday dinner together.

Fifty years ago, it was more usual for a family to have a meal together than it is today. In the past, people usually lived much nearer their work and got home earlier.

I remember...

Stan Taylor is Luke and Sophie's grandfather. His dad was a coal miner. 'My dad worked shifts. If he was home, we all ate together. If he was working, it was just mum who ate with us. Sunday dinner was the most important meal of the week. We always ate together on Sundays.'

STORING FOOD

Sophie is putting a loaf of bread into the freezer.

Mr and Mrs Taylor go to the supermarket once a week to buy food. They store tins and packets in the kitchen cupboards. Foods such as milk, cheese and cold meats are kept in the fridge. Anything they want to keep for a long time is stored in the freezer.

These people look very proud of their new fridge.

Today, almost everyone has a fridge in their home. Fifty years ago, fridges were very expensive. Anyone who had a fridge was thought to be very lucky.

I remember...

There was no fridge in Maureen's home when she was a child. 'We kept our food in a sort of walk-in cupboard, called a larder. There was wire mesh netting on the windows to stop insects flying in. In summer, we stood our bottles of milk in buckets of cold water. But I still remember the horrible taste of warm milk.'

WASHING UP

Luke is loading the dishwasher.

Tea is over and Luke is helping to clear up. The Taylor family have a dishwasher. Luke puts the dirty cups and glasses in the top rack. He places the dirty plates, knives and forks on the bottom rack.

These girls did their washing up by hand.

No one had a dishwasher in their house fifty years ago. These girls washed their dishes in the sink. When the dishes were clean, they placed them on a draining board and then dried them with a tea towel.

I remember...

When Maureen was growing up, there was no running hot water in their house. 'I remember as a little girl helping my mother wash the dishes in an old stoneware sink. The dishes drained on a wooden drainer. My mother had to heat the water in a kettle and then carry it to the sink.'

The Taylors have radiators in every room.

Even when it's cold outside, the Taylors are warm inside their house. Hot water flows through the radiators, warming up the air in the rooms. The water is heated by a gas-fired boiler. An electric pump pushes the water round the radiators.

This family had a coal fire in their living room.

Fifty years ago, most homes had coal fires. Gas fires and electric heaters were becoming popular. They were less work than coal fires and cleaner too. They could be turned on and off quickly.

I remember...

Stan only had coal fires in his house. 'It was my job to bring in the coal from the coalhouse in the yard. Every morning, my mum swept out the ashes from the day before and I laid a new fire. We had no heating upstairs. In winter, my bedroom was freezing. I remember finding frost on the inside of my bedroom windows.'

Luke is cleaning the floor of his bedroom with a vacuum cleaner.

Sophie and Luke tidy and clean their own bedrooms. Mrs Taylor does most of the rest of the housework. The floors and work surfaces we have today are easy to keep clean.

This woman had to clean around her fireplace by hand.

Fifty years ago, coal fires made everything very dusty and dirty. Dusting and polishing took a long time. Some people had vacuum cleaners. Other people used a carpet sweeper or swept the carpet with a brush.

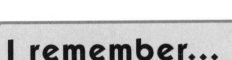

I remember...

Stan remembers how his mum cleaned the carpet. 'She used to sprinkle damp tea leaves on the floor and then sweep them up with a dustpan and brush! She said it kept the dust down. Every spring, she did her spring cleaning. Each room was emptied, everything was washed or cleaned and polished and then it was all put back again.'

ENTERTAINMENT

The Taylors are watching a video on their television set.

The Taylors all enjoy watching television. If they go out, they can video programmes and watch them later. Sometimes, they hire videos from the video library. If they want to hear music, they listen to the radio or play CDs.

This family is getting ready to listen to a radio programme.

Fifty years ago, few people had television sets but almost every family had a radio. There were only three radio stations. People also liked to listen to records on a gramophone.

I remember...

Stan's favourite radio programme was called Children's Hour. 'You always learned something new when you tuned in to Children's Hour. It was interesting but it was fun, too. Fifty years ago, all the programmes were broadcast by the BBC. Today there is much more choice.'

PLAYING INDOORS

Luke and Sophie like playing games together on the computer.

Sophie enjoys adventure games on the computer. Luke prefers car-racing games. They also use the computer to chat with friends around the world on the Internet.

Family board games were very popular fifty years ago.

This family is playing a board game. Few families had a television set, so games were a good way for the whole family to have fun together. There were no home computers fifty years ago.

I remember...

Stan's favourite toy was a clockwork train set. 'I used to lay the set out on my bedroom floor and run the track under my bed. When the train disappeared under the bed, I pretended it was in a tunnel. I also had a stamp collection. I saved up my pocket money to buy packets of stamps from around the world.'

Luke is playing with a radio-controlled car.

Luke and Sophie like playing in their garden. Sophie enjoys playing on the climbing frame. On summer days they take their toys out into the garden. It looks like an outdoor playroom!

These children are playing on a swing.

Fifty years ago, swings were starting to become popular in gardens. But most children would still have had to go to the park if they wanted to play on climbing frames, slides or see-saws.

I remember...

Maureen used to play with the other children who lived in her road. 'We always played together in the street. The roads were much safer then. There were very few cars. We played all sorts of games, like football, skipping, hopscotch and chase.'

The Taylor family used to live hundreds of miles away.

The Taylor family only moved to this house last year. They moved because Mr Taylor got a new job in a different part of the country. The people who used to live next door to Luke and Sophie have come to visit. They haven't seen each other since the Taylor family moved.

These people have moved to a new house close to where they used to live.

Fifty years ago, when people moved home, they did not usually move very far. When couples got married, they often lived near their parents. Most people did not move very often. They might move if they needed a bigger house for their family.

I remember...

Maureen and Stan moved house after their second child was born. 'We didn't have much money, so instead of having proper removal men, one of my father's friends came round in his work van one evening and we moved all the furniture in that.'

NOTES FOR PARENTS

This book is designed to be used on many different levels.

The words in bold provide a simple, core text. The rest of the text provides greater detail, more background information and some personal reminiscences. Competent readers will be able to tackle the entire text themselves. Younger readers could share the reading of the text with an adult. Non-readers will benefit from hearing the text read aloud to them.

All children will enjoy comparing and contrasting the main pictures on each double-page spread. Every picture is a rich resource with much that can be observed and discussed. Ideas for discussion points and questions to ask about each photograph can be found below.

Children are likely to have relatives who will have clear memories of everyday life fifty years ago. There is nothing that brings history to life more vividly than personal recollections. If these memories can be supported by photographs or other artefacts, such as letters, toys or other objects, then the experience is made all the more 'real' to a child.

This particular book is about everyday life at home. You could encourage children to look around their own homes and think about the similarities and differences between homes today and homes fifty years ago. For instance, the basic design of beds has changed very little over fifty years but bedding has changed significantly. Today, most children have duvets on their beds, whereas fifty years ago they would have had sheets, blankets and eiderdowns.

About the Photographs

Washing clothes page 5

Questions to ask:
Which room is this washing machine in?
Does washing clothes look easy?

Points to explore:
Find out which soap powders were available fifty years ago and those which are still available today. Find out how many households now have washing machines compared with fifty years ago.

Ironing page 7

Question to ask:
How does this iron look different to one of today's irons?

Points to discuss:
Discuss how the introduction of man-made fabrics changed the way clothes were washed and ironed. Encourage the understanding that history is not just about 'then' as opposed to 'now' but is a continuous process, by looking back at the development of household appliance designs through the last fifty years.

Cooking page 9

Questions to ask:
What ingredients can you see?
What do you think they are making?

Points to explore:
Discuss our changing cooking habits since the introduction of fridge/freezers, modern electric cookers and microwaves. Compare the healthiness of the food we eat today with the food we ate fifty years ago.

Meal times page 11

Questions to ask:
What did this family drink with their meal?
Who is serving the meal?

Points to explore:
Compare the way this table has been set with the way a table might be set today. Find an old cookery book and see what meals were popular fifty years ago. Discuss the increasing popularity of international food and talk about why that might be.

AND TEACHERS

Storing food page 13

Questions to ask:
How many of the foods in the fridge do we still eat today?
How are things packaged differently now?

Points to explore:
Discover other ways that people tried to keep their food fresh and cool fifty years ago. Find out how different foods, such as flour and salt were stored.

Washing up page 15

Questions to ask:
What are these girls wearing over their dresses?
What is the sink made from?

Points to explore:
Find out about the different ways in which water was heated in homes fifty years ago. Compare the design of kitchens fifty years ago with the design of kitchens today.

Keeping warm page 17

Questions to ask:
At what time of the day do you think this photograph was taken?
What is the boy reading?

Points to explore:
Think about the safety issues connected with open fires. Find out about air pollution and smog.

Housework page 19

Questions to ask:
How is the woman cleaning the fireplace?
What can you see behind the woman?

Points to explore:
Compare the machines we use to clean our homes now with the machines that were available fifty years ago. Discuss the materials that are used in homes today and how much easier they are to keep clean.

Entertainment page 21

Questions to ask:
What sort of clothes are the people in this photograph wearing?
Why is the man turning the knob on the radio?

Points to explore:
Find out why radios were so much larger fifty years ago than they are today. Ask friends and relatives about their favourite radio programmes.

Playing indoors page 23

Questions to ask:
How many people are playing this game?/
Whose turn do you think it is?

Points to explore:
Find out which board games were popular fifty years ago and how many are still available today. Ask friends and relatives whether they played any other games, such as Charades or Murder in the Dark.

Playing outdoors page 25

Questions to ask:
What material is the swing made from?
What is the little girl in the background sitting on?

Points to discuss:
Find out about other popular street games. Discuss why children today do not play in the streets outside their homes as much as they did fifty years ago.

Moving house page 27

Questions to ask:
What sort of furniture can you see in this photograph?
Do you think the people in the picture were well-off or not very well-off?

Points to discuss:
Find out how much houses cost fifty years ago and how much similar houses cost today. Talk about the advantages of families living close together.

GLOSSARY

 **carpet sweeper** A household tool that was pushed over carpets. It had brushes on rollers that picked up the dust.

 **hopscotch** A children's game played by hopping on squares marked out on the ground, usually in chalk.

 **clothes horse** A wooden frame that was used for airing clothes. It could be folded up when it was put away.

 **larder** A small room or large cupboard where food was stored.

 **coalhouse** A small shed where coal was stored.

 **mangle** A machine that was used to squeeze water out of wet clothes.

 **draining board** A kind of tray beside a sink where dishes were put to drip dry once they had been washed.

 **stoneware sink** A sink made from a type of pottery covered with a see-through coating.

 **gramophone** The old word for a record player. Records were called gramophone records when they were first invented.

 **yard** A name sometimes given to the small area behind a house. It was often paved and usually had walls around it.

FURTHER INFORMATION

Books to read

Food Discovered Through History by K. Bryant-Mole
  (A&C Black, 1996)

Home Life in Grandma's Day by F. Gardner (Evans, 1997)

Homes Discovered Through History by K. Bryant-Mole
  (A&C Black, 1996)

Housework by R. Thomson (Watts, 1994)

People at Home by K. Bryant-Mole (Wayland, 1996)

Use this book for teaching literacy

This book can help you in the literacy hour in the following ways:

✓ Children can extend the skills of reading non-fiction. There are two levels of text given, a simple version and a more advanced level.

✓ They can recognise that non-fiction books with similar themes can present similar information in different ways.

✓ They can be encouraged to ask their relatives about their lives when they were children and learn indirectly about history.

✓ They can imagine and write stories about what their lives would have been like fifty years ago, for example, without dishwashers, home computers and television.